AF421811

Dan is excited to show all the fun things he can do! From running fast like the wind to hopping high like a bunny, he's full of energy and imagination. In each colorful scene, Dan explores new activities, like drawing rockets, stacking blocks, and even sharing his bedtime routine. As he tries each new thing, Dan learns that it's not about being perfect—it's about having fun, being proud of yourself, and discovering just how amazing you are! With rhyming text and playful illustrations, this story is perfect for inspiring little ones to explore their own talents.

ALL THE THINGS I CAN DO!

By Dan Farmer

My name is Dan

Look at all the things I can do!

I can put on my own shoes!

One shoe, two shoe. Would you
look at all the things I can do.

Look at all the things I can do!

I can jump as high as that box!

I can jump right over those giant rocks!

Look at all the things I can do!

Look at all the things I can do!

I can draw silly shapes, like circles and stars,

And even a rocket to fly me to Mars!

Just look at all the wonderful things
I can do!

Look at all the things I can do!

I can build with blocks, stack them
so tall,
One, two, three... look, they didn't
fall!

Look at all the things I can do!

I can help tidy up, put my toys in a
row,

Being helpful is something I'm
proud to show.

Look at all the things I can do!

Look at all the things I can do!

I can share!

Sharing is when you trust someone with something
very important to you.

I can share my toys!

I can share my thoughts!

I can even share my feelings so that those who love and support me can help me to better understand them!

I can share when I am sad...

I can share when I am MAD...

I can share when I am glad!

Look at all the things I can do!

Look at all the things I can do!

I can dance with my feet, twirl, wiggle, and sway,

It's fun to move around in my own silly way.

Look at all those crazy cool moves!
Look at all the things I can do!

Look at all the things I can do!

I can ride my bike, pedals go round,

Wheee! Zooming down the street without a sound!

I can ride so fast! The trees are a blur as I pass.
Look at all the things I can do!

Look at all the things I can do!

I can read all by myself, with each page I turn,

Stories about pirates, dragons, and more to learn!

Look at all the things I can do!

I can make animal noises.

Can you?

Let's hear your best Lion!

Now how about an Elephant?

Oh wow, that was great!

Look at all the things WE can do!

Look at all the things we can do!

We can count to 10!

Let's do it together!

2 3 4

5 6 7

8 9 10

Look at all the things we can do!

I can spell my own name,

It is spelled D A N!

Can you spell your own name?

Find the letters to spell your
name in the alphabet on the
next page!

Look at all the things we can do!

A B C D E F G
H I J K L M N
O P Q R S T U
V W X Y Z

Can you write your name in the spaces above?

Look at all the things we can do!

We have a bedtime routine that we
must stick to,

We start with brushing our teeth.

Smile so bright and so clean!

Look at all the things we can do!

Look at all the things we can do!

We can give the best hugs, big and
tight,

Hugs for my friends and family feel
just right.

Let's be sure to give someone
special a big hug good night.

Look at all the things we can do!

Look at all the things we can do!

We can go to bed and sleep soundly all night!

We best get some sleep! Would you like to know
why?

Because tomorrow is a new day full of new THINGS
for us to try!

I am so proud of all the things WE can do.

Hey, looky there! Being proud is something new we can do!

Good night best buddy. Until tomorrow when we can again

Look at all the things we can do!

Loved Dan's adventure?

We'd love to hear from you! Your reviews help other readers discover Look at All the Things I Can Do! and support the creative journey.
If this book made you smile, inspired your little one, or sparked new ideas for fun activities, please take a moment to share your thoughts on Amazon. Your review makes a big difference!

Feel free to post a video review on our amazon page of your little ones showing off "all the things they can do." Let's help our kiddos help each other to build confidence!

Thank you for helping Dan's story reach more young readers! 😊